I0532300

Grass Is Green Where It's

Watered:

The Power of Servant Leadership

By Michelle Murray

Copyright © 2024 Michelle Murray

All rights reserved. This book or any portion thereof may not be reproduced or used in any manner whatsoever without the express written permission of the publisher except for the use of brief quotation in a book review.

Printed in the United States of America

KMP Entertainment (Publishing Division)
www.kmpentertainment.org

Introduction:

Embracing the Heart of Servant Leadership

In a world that often prioritizes power and authority, servant leadership offers a refreshing and life changing approach to leadership. It is a leadership style that is deeply rooted in humility, compassion, and a profound commitment to serving others.

Robert K. Greenleaf coined the term servant leadership in his seminal 1970 essay, "The Servant as Leader." Over the last fifty years or so, this term has greatly influenced modern leadership concepts and practices. Greenleaf was the first to point out to us that not only can servanthood and leadership merge together in one person, but that it is a must to be most impactful and effective.

As an Army Veteran, I have observed and studied countless leaders who have embraced the heart of servant leadership. This type of leader always has a remarkable impact on the people and the world around them. Why? Servant leadership is much more than a surface-level philosophy. It is a profound and holistic way of being that shapes every aspect of a leader's life. It challenges the conventional notion of leadership as a position of authority and control, shifting the focus toward selflessness, empathy, and ensuring the well-being of those they serve. At the core of servant leadership lies the art of deep listening.

Servant leaders understand that effective leadership begins with a genuine desire to understand the perspectives, needs, and aspirations of those they lead. They go beyond surface-level conversations, immersing themselves in active listening, seeking to truly hear and comprehend the voices of their team members. By creating an environment that values open and honest communication, servant leaders build trust, strengthen relationships, and foster a culture of authentic connection.

In addition to actively listening, servant leaders cultivate empathy as a foundational tenet of their leadership approach. They put themselves in the shoes of others, recognizing the value and uniqueness of each person's experience. By embracing empathy, servant leaders are able to nurture meaningful connections and create an inclusive environment where individuals feel valued, appreciated, and understood.

Servant leaders prioritize the holistic well-being of their team members. They understand the importance of fostering a sense of psychological safety, where individuals feel comfortable being themselves and expressing their thoughts and ideas without fear of judgment or retribution. By cultivating an atmosphere of trust and support, servant leaders empower their followers to take risks, grow, and contribute their best work. They attend to both the personal and professional growth of their team members, understanding that a fulfilled and nurtured individual will be more engaged and dedicated to their work.

Mindfulness and self-awareness also play roles in the servant leadership journey. Servant leaders recognize the power of being fully present in every moment, grounding themselves in the here and now. By practicing mindfulness, they cultivate a heightened sense of self-awareness, enabling them to lead with intention, authenticity, and emotional intelligence. They are attuned to their own strengths and limitations, constantly seeking personal growth and development.

Servant leaders are visionary persuaders, capable of inspiring others through their compelling visions for the future. They paint a vivid picture of what could be, igniting passion and commitment within their teams. Understanding the importance of collective purpose, servant leaders ensure their visions align with the needs and aspirations of their followers, inspiring a sense of shared ownership and involvement in the journey toward their shared goals. They possess the ability to anticipate change, conceptualize ideas, and effectively communicate their vision, rallying others to join in the pursuit of a shared purpose.

At the heart of servant leadership is the concept of stewardship. Servant leaders embrace the idea that they are the custodians of their organization's resources, entrusted with the responsibility of using them wisely and ethically. They approach decision-making with a long-term perspective, considering the impact on not just the present, but also the future. Servant leaders recognize their responsibility to preserve and nurture the natural environment, seeking sustainable practices that honor the interconnectedness between humanity and the planet. They invest in the development and growth of their team members, understanding that by empowering others, they create a ripple effect of positive change that extends far beyond their own leadership tenure. Lastly, servant leaders understand the power of building a community within their organizations. They emphasize collaboration, cooperation, and a deep sense of belonging among their team members.

By creating a space where discourse is welcome, servant leaders foster an environment where different opinions are valued and differing perspectives are embraced. They encourage active participation, seeking to create a collective sense of purpose and shared responsibility. Servant leaders foster a strong team culture that supports innovation, creativity, and continuous learning, ensuring that everyone's voices are heard and contributions are valued.

Throughout this book, we will delve deeply into each aspect of servant leadership, drawing on inspiring examples from past and present servant leaders who have made lasting impacts in their respective fields. We will explore practical strategies, tools, and insights that can help leaders embody and integrate servant leadership into their daily lives. By embracing the heart of servant leadership, we can collectively create a world where leadership is seen not as a position of power, but as a noble privilege to serve and uplift others. Together, let us embark on this journey, unlocking the incredible potential within ourselves to become servant leaders who make a positive and lasting impact on the lives of those around us.

The Essence of Servant Leadership

Servant leadership, a timeless philosophy and practice, goes beyond the conventional notion of leadership by imbuing it with compassion, empathy, and a deep commitment to serving others. At its core, servant leadership goes beyond transactional relationships and embraces a transformative approach that not only benefits individuals but also the collective as a whole.

Embodying servant leadership requires a fundamental shift in mindset and perspective. It starts with recognizing that leadership is not about exerting control or wielding power over others, but rather about harnessing influence to uplift and empower them. Read that last sentence again. Then chew on it a moment before you proceed.

Servant leaders understand that their role is to serve, guide, and enable others to unlock their full potential. One crucial element woven into the fabric of servant leadership is active listening. It is not merely about passively hearing words, but rather engaging fully with the speaker, offering undivided attention, and embracing a genuine curiosity to comprehend their thoughts, emotions, and motivations.

Through active listening, servant leaders create a safe space for open dialogue, fostering trust and mutual understanding. In addition to active listening, servant leaders lead with empathy and compassion. They seek to understand the unique challenges, aspirations, and fears of their team members, recognizing that each individual has their own story and journey. By cultivating empathy, leaders can foster deeper connections, forge authentic relationships, and demonstrate genuine care for the well-being of their team.

Servant leaders should develop a holistic view of their team members, understanding that they are not just employees but whole individuals with diverse experiences, skills, and aspirations. Unlike other leaders, servant leaders create opportunities for professional and personal development, recognizing that investing in the growth of their team members not only benefits the individual but also enhances the overall team and organizational performance. While servant leadership emphasizes the needs of others, it also entails a commitment to personal growth and continuous learning.

True servant leaders recognize that they must continually develop their own skills, knowledge, and emotional intelligence in order to better serve those they lead. They invest in self-reflection, seek feedback, and actively pursue self-improvement. By expanding their own horizons, leaders set an example and inspire their team members to embark on their own journeys of growth and mastery. Moreover, servant leaders foster collaboration and unity within their teams. They dismantle hierarchical barriers and cultivate an inclusive environment where diverse perspectives are valued.

Through effective communication, collaboration, and collective decision-making, servant leaders tap into the collective intelligence and creativity of their team, leading to innovative solutions and achieving shared goals. Servant leaders also possess deep humility, acknowledging that they do not have all the answers and that their purpose is not to control or command, but to serve alongside their team members. They embrace vulnerability, recognizing that admitting mistakes and seeking input from others strengthens their leadership and encourages a culture of honesty and openness. Additionally, servant leaders exhibit a strong sense of ethical responsibility. They prioritize the well-being of their team members, customers, and stakeholders above personal gain. They make decisions that are in alignment with the organization's values and mission, always considering the long-term impact on the greater community.

By acting with integrity and transparency, servant leaders inspire trust and loyalty in their teams.

Ultimately, the essence of servant leadership lies in the authentic desire to make a positive impact on the lives of others. Servant leaders view their role as a stewardship, understanding that their influence extends far beyond the workplace. They nurture and support the holistic well-being of their team members by fostering a healthy work-life balance, promoting personal development, and caring for their physical and emotional welfare. In conclusion, servant leadership is a profound and transformative approach that challenges traditional views of leadership. It requires embodying qualities such as active listening, empathy, humility, and a commitment to personal and collective growth. By embracing servant leadership, individuals can ignite positive change in organizations, communities, and society at large, creating a ripple effect of compassion, empowerment, and sustainable success.

Listening: The Foundation of Connection

In the realm of leadership, few skills are as important or often overlooked as the ability to truly listen. In our fast-paced, information-driven world, where everyone seems to have something to say, listening can easily be overshadowed by the need to be heard. Yet, it is through listening that we forge deep connections, understanding, and trust with those we lead.

As a leader, listening becomes the foundation upon which all other aspects of leadership are built. Listening is not merely hearing the words spoken by others; it is a multifaceted and nuanced process that requires intentionality, empathy, and an open heart. It is about being fully present and engaged in the conversation, creating a space where individuals feel valued and heard.

Research has shown that active listening is the key to effective communication, conflict resolution, and organizational success. Effective listening requires patience and practice. It is a skill that can be cultivated and honed over time, and its benefits are immeasurable. When leaders truly listen, they gain valuable insights, foster stronger relationships, and create an inclusive and collaborative culture.

Here are some key principles to keep in mind as we embark on the journey of mastering the art of listening:

1. Create a place where thinking is encouraged:

As a leader, it is essential to create an environment where people encouraged and comfortable expressing themselves. When individuals trust that their ideas, concerns, and emotions will be respected, they are more likely to open up and share their thoughts openly. Encouraging open communication and actively seeking different or even opposing viewpoints allows for a richer and more comprehensive understanding of the challenges and opportunities we face.

2. Be Fully Present:

In a world filled with distractions and divided attention, truly listening requires our undivided focus and presence. This means putting aside smartphones, laptops, and other distractions, and truly committing ourselves to the conversation at hand. By giving our full attention, we send a powerful message that we value and respect the person speaking, fostering an environment where individuals feel heard and acknowledged. Active listening involves not only hearing the words but also paying attention to the speaker's tone, body language, and emotions. This holistic approach to listening allows us to gather more information and truly understand the underlying message being conveyed.

3. Suspend Assumptions:

As humans, we bring our own preconceived notions and frame of references to a conversation. To truly listen, we must set these aside and approach each interaction with an open mind. Recognizing and challenging our own paradigms allows us to genuinely hear and understand the speaker's perspective, even if it differs from our own. This practice not only enhances our understanding but also cultivates an environment where different ideas can flourish and innovation can thrive.

Active listening involves active questioning – asking open-ended questions that invite the speaker to elaborate and provide more insight. By seeking clarification and asking probing questions, we demonstrate our commitment to understanding, fostering deeper connections, and encouraging critical thinking.

4. Practice Active Listening:

Listening goes beyond hearing the words spoken; it involves actively engaging with the speaker to understand their intentions, emotions, and needs. Active listening requires not only paying attention to verbal cues but also being attuned to nonverbal cues, such as body language and facial expressions. By observing and interpreting these cues, we can gain a more complete understanding of the speaker's message and emotional state. To demonstrate our active engagement, we can paraphrase or summarize what we have heard, seeking clarification or confirmation from the speaker. This demonstrates that we are fully present, attentive, and committed to comprehending their message.

5. Show Empathy and Compassion:

Listening is not just about understanding the facts; it is about connecting with the emotions and experiences behind the words. Empathy and compassion play a crucial role in effective listening, as they help us truly relate to others and build meaningful connections. By seeking to understand and validate the emotions expressed by the speaker, we validate their experiences and allow vulnerability, fostering trust and strengthening relationships.

Active listening includes responding empathetically to the speaker, acknowledging their emotions and perspective. This validates their feelings and encourages them to share more openly, leading to deeper connections and better problem-solving. By embracing the art of listening, leaders can foster an atmosphere of trust, collaboration, and innovation. When people feel heard and valued, they are more likely to contribute their best work, engage wholeheartedly in the organization's mission, and feel a sense of purpose and belonging.

As leaders, let us remember that our role is not just to speak and direct, but to listen and understand. By making listening a priority, we can build bridges of connection, inspire greatness in others, and create a culture of shared purpose and achievement.

Empathy: Understanding and Valuing Others

Embracing empathy is a fundamental aspect of servant leadership. It is the ability to authentically understand and truly value the thoughts, feelings, and experiences of others at a profound level. When we genuinely empathize with those we lead, we create a culture of trust, compassion, and respect that transcends surface-level interactions. At its core, empathy is about putting ourselves in someone else's shoes and striving to comprehend the world through their lens.

Empathy goes beyond sympathy, which is feeling pity or sorrow for someone's plight. Empathy is about actively seeking to understand the emotional landscape of others and acknowledging the validity of their experiences. The practice of empathy begins with active listening, a skill that requires patience, attention, and an open heart. It involves setting aside our own thoughts, judgements, and biases, and fully immersing ourselves in the present moment to engage with another person.

When we actively listen, we not only focus on the words being spoken but also attune ourselves to the underlying emotions and unspoken messages. We become aware of the tone, body language, and facial expressions that provide valuable insight into someone's internal state. By truly listening, without interrupting or imposing our agenda, we create space for deep connection and understanding.

To deepen our empathetic abilities, we must keenly observe and interpret non-verbal cues. Facial expressions, gestures, and body language often communicate unexpressed emotions that can shape the meaning behind someone's words. A furrowed brow may indicate concern, while an excited hand gesture can reveal enthusiasm. By honing our observation skills, we can discern when someone seems uncomfortable, anxious, or genuinely interested, even if they don't explicitly state it. This awareness allows us to respond with compassion and provides an opportunity to foster a supportive environment for open communication.

Valuing others is a crucial component of empathy. It means recognizing the inherent worth, dignity, and contributions of each individual. As servant leaders, we understand that every person's unique qualities and perspectives enrich the collective experience of the team. By embracing diversity, we create a tapestry of ideas that leads to innovation, creativity, and exponential growth. By actively valuing and celebrating differences, we establish an inclusive culture that encourages collaboration, respect, and appreciation.

In addition to understanding emotions, empathy involves validating the experiences of others. It means acknowledging their perspective and offering support without offense or defensiveness. Validation often requires us to step out of our own perspective and wholeheartedly embrace someone else's point of view. It may require shifting our paradigms a bit to truly understand someone's perspective. By creating an empathetic atmosphere for individuals to express their thoughts and feelings, free from fear of ridicule or reprisal, we foster an environment where each person feels seen, heard, and understood.

Practicing empathy also requires us to anticipate the needs, challenges, and desires of those we lead. By placing ourselves in their shoes, we develop a heightened sensitivity to their unique circumstances, hopes, and fears. This understanding enables us to provide appropriate resources, guidance, and support. Proactively addressing their needs demonstrates our commitment to their growth and well-being, fostering trust and loyalty within the team.

To deepen our empathetic abilities, we must continually engage in self-reflection. We need to examine our own paradigms, assumptions, and any unconscious preconceptions that may hinder our ability to truly connect with others. By becoming aware of our own limitations and actively seeking to expand our understanding, we become more effective and compassionate servant leaders.

Ultimately, empathy is a lifelong journey of growth and understanding. It is not merely a box to check, but an impactful way of being in the world and leading others. By prioritizing empathy in our daily interactions, we create a ripple effect that extends beyond the workplace. We become catalysts for positive change, promoting empathy and understanding in the broader community. Empathy is the cornerstone of servant leadership. It requires active listening, observation, valuing others, validation, and anticipation of needs. By cultivating deep empathy, we foster a culture of trust, compassion, and respect, resulting in a high-performing and cohesive team. Through empathy, we have the power to improve relationships, organizations, and the world.

Healing: Nurturing Emotional Well-being

One of the most vital aspects of servant leadership is the ability to heal and nurture emotional maturity and well-being. Emotions are intricately woven into the fabric of our lives, shaping our thoughts, behaviors, and overall experiences. As leaders, understanding and addressing the emotional needs of others can have a profound impact on their growth and development, as well as the overall success of the team or organization. To effectively heal and foster emotional well-being, it is essential to create a supportive environment where individuals feel seen, heard, and valued. This begins with active and empathetic listening, a skill that requires a deep level of attentiveness and presence. It entails not only hearing the words being spoken but also understanding the underlying emotions that accompany them. By truly listening and acknowledging these emotions, leaders can build trust and establish a solid foundation for healing.

Empathy, the capacity to understand and share the feelings of another, is a powerful tool in healing emotional wounds. It involves stepping into someone else's shoes and seeing the world from their perspective. When leaders demonstrate empathy, they show their genuine care and concern for those they lead. This fosters a sense of belonging and helps individuals feel supported and understood, even during times of difficulty. When people know that their emotions are acknowledged and respected, they are more likely to open up, express themselves authentically, and engage fully in their work.

Emotional maturity goes beyond just listening and empathizing; it also necessitates providing the necessary resources and support for individuals to address their emotional struggles. This can take various forms, depending on the specific needs of the individual and the circumstances at hand. It may involve offering counseling services or establishing employee assistance programs, creating spaces for open dialogue and emotional expression, or organizing workshops on emotional intelligence and self-care.

By investing in the emotional well-being of their team members, leaders create an environment where individuals feel empowered to explore their emotions, seek help when needed, and grow both personally and professionally. Developing emotional maturity in subordinates requires leaders to lead by example. By sharing their own struggles and lessons learned, leaders create a space for others to do the same. This openness fosters a culture of trust and psychological safety, where individuals feel comfortable expressing their emotions without fear of judgment or retribution.

By embracing vulnerability, leaders not only deepen their connection with their team members but also cultivate an environment where emotions are embraced as an integral part of the human experience. It is important to recognize that emotional maturity and emotional healing are ongoing processes. They both require consistent effort and attention to ensure that individuals feel supported and empowered to navigate their emotions productively. Leaders must be proactive in their approach, regularly checking in with their team members, and providing continuous opportunities for growth and healing.

This may involve refining communication strategies, enhancing conflict resolution skills, or promoting self-care practices that allow individuals to recharge and rejuvenate. By fostering a sense of community and shared purpose, leaders can create an environment where individuals come together, support one another, and collectively celebrate successes and navigate challenges.

Healing and maturity of emotions at this level strengthens the bonds between team members, enhances collaboration, and ultimately fuels the team's ability to achieve their goals. To foster healing and emotional maturity, leaders can also incorporate various practices into their leadership approach. Mindfulness, for example, can be a powerful tool in promoting self-awareness and emotional regulation. Encouraging individuals to engage in mindfulness exercises, such as meditation or deep breathing, can help them manage stress, reduce anxiety, and enhance their overall emotional well-being. By incorporating mindfulness practices into the organizational culture, leaders create an environment that values self-reflection and self-care.

Promoting a sense of purpose and meaning can foster emotional well-being within a team or organization. When individuals feel connected to a larger purpose beyond themselves, their work becomes more fulfilling and meaningful. Leaders can emphasize the significance of the team's mission, creating a shared sense of purpose that inspires individuals to contribute their best efforts. By aligning the tasks and objectives of the team with their personal values and aspirations, leaders help cultivate a sense of passion and emotional fulfillment that sustains individuals through difficult times.

In addition to these practices, leaders can also facilitate opportunities for personal growth and development. Emotional well-being is closely tied to individual growth and a sense of progress. By providing ongoing training, mentoring programs, or opportunities to stretch and challenge themselves, leaders empower individuals to continuously learn and develop their emotional resilience. Nurturing a growth mindset within the team or organization can promote emotional well-being by encouraging individuals to embrace failures as learning experiences and view challenges as opportunities for growth.

It is crucial for leaders to foster a culture of appreciation and recognition. Positive emotions play a significant role in emotional well-being of the team and the individual, and by acknowledging and celebrating the achievements and efforts of team members, leaders create an environment that cultivates positivity. Expressing gratitude and recognizing the contributions of individuals not only promotes their emotional well-being but also strengthens the bonds within the team, enhancing collaboration and overall team performance.

Healing and nurturing emotional maturity and well-being is a fundamental aspect of servant leadership. By actively listening, demonstrating empathy, providing resources and support, modeling vulnerability, incorporating mindfulness practices, promoting a sense of purpose, facilitating personal growth, and fostering a culture of appreciation, leaders can create an environment where individuals feel seen, heard, and valued. When emotional healing is prioritized, teams become more cohesive, resilient, and capable of achieving their fullest potential. Truly embracing and caring for the emotional well-being of their team members is not just a responsibility for servant leaders, but a meaningful and essential act that fosters growth and propels the organization forward.

Mindfulness and Awareness: Cultivating Presence

In a world filled with constant distractions and overwhelming demands, cultivating presence through mindfulness and awareness is essential for effective leadership. Mindfulness is the practice of being fully present in the moment, embracing each experience with a non-judgmental attitude. When leaders cultivate mindfulness, they create a space for deeper connection, understanding, and decision-making. To cultivate mindfulness, leaders must first learn to be fully present in each moment.

This means letting go of concerns about the past or future and instead focusing on the here and now. By redirecting their attention to the present, leaders can tune into the nuances of their environment and the emotions of their team members. This level of awareness allows leaders to make more informed decisions and respond appropriately to the needs of their team. One technique to enhance mindfulness is through meditation.

Allocating regular time for meditation helps train the mind to focus on the present moment and cultivate a sense of calm. Sitting in stillness and observing the breath or engaging in guided imagery can help quiet the mind and create space for deeper self-awareness. Through consistent meditation practice, leaders can increase their ability to be present with their team, fostering healthier relationships and improved communication.

Another powerful tool in the cultivation of mindfulness and awareness is mindfulness-based stress reduction (MBSR). This structured program, developed by Jon Kabat-Zinn, combines mindfulness meditation with exercise. MBSR has been shown to reduce stress, increase self-awareness, and enhance overall well-being. By participating in such an exercise program, leaders can develop a deep understanding of their own stress triggers and learn how to respond to them with greater equanimity. Awareness, on the other hand, involves a deep understanding of oneself and the impact that one's thoughts, emotions, and actions have on others.

Cultivating awareness requires leaders to engage in self-reflection and introspection, exploring their strengths, weaknesses, and paradigms. By examining their beliefs and paradigms, leaders can uncover hidden assumptions that may unintentionally influence their decision-making processes. This heightened self-awareness allows leaders to make conscious choices that are aligned with their values and the greater good.

Self-reflection can take many forms. Leaders may journal about their experiences, seeking patterns and themes. They may engage in mindfulness exercises that invite them to observe their thoughts and emotions without judgment. They can also seek feedback from trusted advisors or participate in coaching or leadership development programs to deepen their self-awareness. The key is to invest time and effort into self-exploration, as it lays the foundation for becoming a mindful and aware leader.

By combining mindfulness and awareness, leaders can foster a sense of presence that allows them to respond thoughtfully and empathetically to the needs of their team. This presence enables leaders to tap into their intuition and make decisions that align with their values and the greater good. It also allows them to recognize the potential of others and provide the necessary support and guidance to help them grow and flourish.

Practicing mindfulness and awareness is not an easy task, especially in today's fast-paced environment. However, it is a skill that can be developed through regular practice and self-discipline. Leaders can also seek support from mindfulness-based programs or engage in professional coaching to enhance their mindfulness and awareness skills. In addition to meditation and self-reflection, practicing gratitude can further deepen mindfulness and awareness. Expressing appreciation and recognizing the positive aspects of life and work fosters a mindset of abundance and contentment. Leaders who cultivate gratitude create a positive and supportive work culture, encouraging their team members to feel valued and engaged.

Incorporating mindfulness into daily tasks and activities can help leaders maintain their sense of presence. For example, practicing mindful eating involves savoring each bite, paying attention to the flavors, textures, and sensations. Engaging in mindful walking or exercise involves fully experiencing the movement of the body and the sensations that arise. By infusing moments throughout the day with mindfulness, leaders can enhance their overall well-being and the quality of their interactions.

By embracing mindfulness and awareness, leaders create an environment of trust, compassion, and authenticity. They become present to the needs of their team members, fostering collaboration and innovation. Through cultivating presence, leaders can navigate challenges with wisdom and grace, inspiring and empowering those around them. In the next chapter, we will explore the power of persuasion and how leaders can influence others through inspiration and genuine connection.

Persuasion: Influencing Through Inspiration

Leaders are tasked to provide purpose, direction and motivation to their teams. So, it goes without saying that a leader's influence plays a vital role in shaping the direction and success of both individuals and organizations. True leadership, though, is not about exerting power or control over others. It is about inspiring and persuading them to voluntarily align their actions with a shared vision and common goals.

Persuasion, when rooted in inspiration, is the key to igniting this impactful leadership. It is the art of guiding others through the power of influence and compelling ideas, rather than relying on authority or coercion. By inspiring those we lead, we can tap into their intrinsic motivation and unleash their full potential. To effectively persuade, one must first connect deeply with others.

This requires active listening, empathy, and a genuine understanding of their needs, desires, and aspirations. When we take the time to truly know and value those we lead, we can craft persuasive messages that resonate with their values and goals. Active listening goes beyond just hearing the words spoken. It involves paying attention to nonverbal cues, deciphering emotions behind words, and empathizing with the speaker's perspective. Through active listening, leaders can gain valuable insights into the concerns, challenges, and motivations of their audience, enabling them to tailor their message accordingly.

Empathy is another essential skill in persuasion. It entails putting oneself in the shoes of others and seeing the world from their perspective. When leaders empathize with those they wish to influence, they can better understand their fears, aspirations, and desires, allowing them to frame their message in a way that resonates deeply. Empathy begins with understanding, acknowledging, and validating the emotions and experiences of others. Leaders can foster trust and build strong relationships through empathy.

This foundation of trust sets the stage for effective persuasion, as individuals are more likely to be receptive to messages when they feel seen, heard, and respected. But persuasion goes beyond simply conveying information. It involves storytelling, painting vivid pictures of possibility, and tapping into the emotions and aspirations of our audience. People are emotionally-driven beings, and when we appeal to their hearts as well as their minds, we create a connection that fosters trust and inspires action.

Effective storytelling requires a strategic approach. Leaders must understand their audience's values, beliefs, and even their backgrounds to craft compelling communications that resonate. By sharing relatable anecdotes, personal experiences, or relaying the stories of others, leaders can create a sense of shared identity and purpose. The power of storytelling lies in its ability to draw on universal human experiences, creating a collective understanding that overcomes differences.

An effective leader knows how to communicate with charisma and authenticity. They have the ability to build trust and credibility, leading others to willingly follow their lead. By embodying their values and their vision, leaders inspire confidence in their ideas and the path they propose. Building trust and credibility requires consistent, truthful and transparent communication. Leaders must be willing to share both successes and failures, fostering an environment of openness and vulnerability. When leaders are open about their own journey, it encourages others to be more receptive to their influence.

Influencing through inspiration also requires a deep sense of conviction and belief in the vision being shared. When leaders have unwavering faith in their mission and purpose, it becomes contagious. Their enthusiasm and passion become infectious, lighting a fire within others and compelling them to act. However, persuasion should not be mistaken for manipulation or coercion.

True leaders understand the importance of ethical influence and always act with integrity. They respect the autonomy and individuality of others, providing them with the freedom to make their own choices while gently guiding them toward alignment with the greater purpose. Effective persuasion requires adaptability and flexibility in communication styles. Different individuals have unique preferences and ways of processing information. Leaders who can adapt their communication to meet the needs of various personalities and learning styles can make a profound impact on their audience.

It is also essential for leaders to master the art of emotional intelligence. Emotional intelligence involves recognizing and managing their own emotions, as well as understanding the emotions of others. By attuning themselves to the emotional climate of their team or organization, leaders can respond appropriately and address concerns or challenges in a way that fosters trust and engagement. Ultimately, the art of persuasion rests in the ability to build a compelling case and create a sense of urgency and importance. It involves framing the message in a way that aligns with the values and aspirations of others, emphasizing the benefits and positive outcomes that can be achieved by embracing the shared vision.

In the pursuit of servant leadership, persuasion becomes a powerful tool to move others toward a collective purpose, as well as empowerment. Through inspiration, empathy, and a genuine desire to foster growth and collaboration, we can become persuasive leaders who inspire others to unleash their inherent potential and create a better future together. By continuously refining our persuasive skills and exploring innovative ways to connect with and influence those around us, we lay the foundation for a thriving, empowered, and inspired community.

Creating a Compelling Vision

One of the key responsibilities an exceptional leader holds is the ability to create and communicate a compelling vision that resonates deeply with individuals. A compelling vision is a powerful narrative that ignites a profound sense of purpose and possibility within each team member. At its core, a compelling vision is not simply about the leader's personal aspirations or goals, but rather about aligning the collective efforts of the team toward a common goal.

This process begins with the leader engaging in deep reflection and introspection, challenging their own values, beliefs, and dreams. By doing so, they are able to forge a genuine connection between their personal insights and the larger purpose of the organization, allowing them to craft a vision that is authentic, meaningful, and inspiring. To create a vision that captivates hearts and minds, an effective leader understands that it should surpass a mere arrangement of words. It ought to encapsulate a clear, concise, and future-oriented picture of what the organization strives to achieve.

A compelling vision is more than just a snapshot. It should evoke deep emotions within individuals, stirring their imagination and kindling a burning desire to contribute. It becomes a rallying point, inspiring individuals to go above and beyond their usual limitations, driving them to reach new heights of excellence. A compelling vision should be grounded in the realities of the present while providing a well-defined roadmap for future possibilities. By painting a vivid and detailed picture of what success looks like, a visionary leader offers clarity, enabling individuals to visualize the outcome and understand how their efforts contribute to the overall purpose. This understanding helps individuals develop a stronger sense of ownership and commitment toward the vision, fostering a collective determination to overcome challenges and achieve the desired future state.

An essential ingredient in creating a compelling vision is effective communication. A servant leader must be skilled at articulating the vision in a way that resonates with others and captures their hearts and minds. They must use language that is inspiring, and accessible to every member of the team, eliminating any barriers to understanding. By utilizing storytelling techniques, metaphors, and vivid imagery, a leader can bring the vision to life, connecting with individuals on an emotional level, and infusing the vision with their collective hopes, dreams, and aspirations. However, the creation of a compelling vision should not be a one-way street.

A servant leader understands the importance of seeking feedback and being open to adaptation as circumstances evolve. They recognize that the collective wisdom of the team is a valuable resource, and they foster an environment where everyone feels encouraged to share their thoughts and ideas. This exchange of perspectives enriches the vision, making it more robust, dynamic, and responsive to the ever-changing world.

A visionary leader understands their responsibility to lead by example and embody the aspirations and values inherent in the vision they have created. They recognize that words alone are insufficient; action is essential. By consistently aligning their own conduct with the vision they have articulated, they become a source of inspiration and motivation for others. Their unwavering commitment to the vision breeds trust and confidence among team members, empowering them to embrace the vision and strive toward its realization.

Creating a compelling vision is not merely a critical aspect; it is the very essence of servant leadership. A servant leader recognizes that a vision is not just a statement, but a powerful force that unifies individuals, creates synergy, shapes organizational culture, and drives positive change. By engaging in deep reflection, communicating effectively, seeking feedback, and leading by example, a servant leader can create a vision that not only inspires but also transforms the lives of those they serve.

Foresight: Anticipating and Responding to Change

The ability to foresee and adapt to change is a critical skill. The world is constantly evolving, and as leaders, we must be proactive in our approach to anticipate and respond to these changes. This is where the concept of foresight comes into play. Foresight is not just about being vaguely aware of potential disruptions. It involves a comprehensive understanding of internal and external factors shaping our environment. It requires a deep dive into market research, competitor analysis, and consumer insights to identify emerging trends and patterns. This rigorous analysis provides the foundation for informed decision-making and strategic planning.

In today's digital age, where information is readily available and innovation is at an all-time high, leaders need to be more adept at processing and synthesizing vast amounts of data. They must possess the ability to discern meaningful insights from noise. This is where analytical thinking and data-driven decision-making become crucial tools in a leader's arsenal. However, foresight is not solely about quantitative data and analytical frameworks. It also encompasses intuitive thinking and the ability to connect seemingly unrelated dots.

This holistic approach allows leaders to tap into their innate sense of curiosity and creativity, enabling them to envision possibilities and identify potential disruptions before they occur. The process of developing foresight begins with fostering a learning mindset. Leaders must commit to continuous education, staying well-read, attending conferences, and engaging in thought-provoking discussions to broaden their perspectives. By seeking out diverse opinions and challenging their own paradigms, leaders create an environment conducive to innovation and insight.

Leaders must build a strong network of mentors, advisors, and subject matter experts who can provide guidance and offer different viewpoints. This support system acts as a sounding board, helping leaders navigate complexities and validate their foresight strategies. Anticipating change is just the first step; leaders must also possess the flexibility and agility to respond effectively. This requires embracing a culture of adaptability and experimentation.

Leaders must foster an environment where failure is seen as an opportunity for growth and learning rather than a source of shame or blame. This mindset encourages their teams to take calculated risks and explore new ideas, knowing that even if they stumble, they can bounce back stronger. Leaders need to cultivate the ability to communicate their foresight effectively. They must not only articulate the vision but also inspire their teams to embrace change and actively participate in shaping the future.

Through effective storytelling and clear communication, leaders can align their team's purpose, values, and goals with the evolving landscape. In times of uncertainty and turbulence, the leader with foresight is like a lighthouse guiding their organization through the storm. They inspire confidence, instill trust, and provide a clear vision for the future. By anticipating and responding to change, they are better positioned to navigate challenges, seize opportunities, and steer their organization toward long-term success.

Developing the trait of foresight takes time and practice. It requires a deep understanding of one's industry, an ability to scan the horizon for potential disruptions, and the courage to embrace change. It is a skill that can be honed with experience and by surrounding oneself with a people who have a wide variety of experience and backgrounds. To develop foresight, leaders should consider the different dimensions of change.

There are internal changes that may arise from shifts in organizational structure, culture, or processes. Leaders must analyze their organization's strengths and weaknesses, identify areas for improvement, and proactively develop strategies to adapt and remain competitive. Leaders must also be attuned to external changes that impact their industry and market. This includes monitoring technological advancements, regulatory shifts, and social and cultural transformations.

By staying informed and constantly scanning the external environment, leaders can spot emerging trends, identify potential disruptors, and position their organization ahead of the curve. Foresight requires leaders to broaden their perspective beyond short-term goals and focus on long-term implications. While short-term successes are important, leaders must keep an eye on the bigger picture and consider the potential consequences of their actions.

This forward-thinking approach enables leaders to make strategic decisions that align with their organization's long-term vision and goals. In addition to anticipating change, leaders must also be prepared to respond swiftly and effectively. This necessitates agile decision-making and the ability to mobilize resources efficiently. Leaders should establish clear communication channels, develop contingency plans, and empower their teams to take ownership of their roles and responsibilities.

Maintaining open and transparent communication with stakeholders is another crucial component of foresight. By involving employees, customers, partners, and other relevant parties in the strategic planning process, leaders can create a shared vision and gain insights that help inform their decision-making. This collaborative approach fosters a sense of ownership and commitment among stakeholders, ensuring a smoother transition during times of change.

It is important for leaders to constantly evaluate and reassess their foresight strategies. Acknowledging that change is constant, leaders should regularly review their assumptions, challenge their existing paradigms, and adjust their strategies as needed. This continuous improvement mindset enables leaders to stay agile and adaptive, ensuring that their foresight remains relevant in an ever-evolving landscape. Foresight is an essential skill for leaders to thrive in a dynamic world. Cultivating foresight involves a proactive approach to understanding internal and external factors, embracing a learning mindset, fostering adaptability, promoting effective communication, and continuously evaluating and improving strategies. By developing this skill, leaders can effectively navigate change, capitalize on emerging opportunities, and lead their organizations to enduring success.

Stewardship: Guiding with Responsibility

Stewardship plays a crucial role in guiding and nurturing others. It is the recognition and acceptance of the responsibility entrusted to us as leaders, to care for and inspire our team members, the organization, and the community at large. To be a steward means more than just managing resources and making decisions. It requires a deep understanding of the impact our actions have on those around us and the world we live in. As a servant leader, we must embrace this responsibility wholeheartedly and prioritize the well-being of others above all else.

One of the key aspects of stewardship is the careful and ethical use of resources. As leaders, we are entrusted with various forms of resources, whether they are financial, human, or environmental. It is our duty to manage these resources diligently, ensuring their sustainability. This involves not only optimizing efficiency and minimizing waste but also considering the broader implications of our resource allocation decisions.

Financial resources encompass not only revenue and fund allocation, but also investments in growth, innovation, and long-term sustainability. It is our responsibility to make informed decisions that balance short-term goals with the organization's financial health. By managing resources prudently, we can minimize financial risks and secure a stable future for the organization and its stakeholders.

Human resources are the lifeblood of any organization. As stewards, we must recognize the immense value our team members bring and seek to create a nurturing and empowering environment for their growth and well-being. This involves providing opportunities for professional development, and promoting work-life balance. By investing in the personal and professional growth of our team members, we not only enhance their individual skills but also cultivate a motivated and high-performing workforce.

Environmental resources encompass the natural environment in which our organizations operate. As responsible stewards, we have a duty to minimize our ecological footprint and contribute positively to the preservation and restoration of the environment. This calls for adopting sustainable practices throughout our operations, such as reducing carbon emissions, conserving energy and water, and integrating eco-friendly materials and technologies. By doing so, we contribute to the larger goal of ensuring a thriving and sustainable planet for future generations.

Stewardship goes beyond mere resource management, though. It also encompasses nurturing a culture of accountability and transparency within the organization. A responsible steward sets clear expectations and communicates openly with their team members, fostering an environment of trust and integrity. This includes establishing a feedback system that encourages open and honest communication, recognizing and rewarding achievements, but also addressing concerns or issues promptly.

By holding ourselves and others accountable, we create a space where individuals take ownership of their actions and collaborate for collective success. However, true stewardship is not limited to our immediate environment. As servant leaders, we recognize that we are also stewards of the larger community. We have a responsibility to contribute positively to the well-being of society as a whole.

This may involve supporting local charities and non-profit organizations, engaging in community development projects, or advocating for those in the community. By actively seeking ways to serve and give back, we not only impact individual lives but enhance the community's overall viability.

In addition to resource management and community engagement, stewardship involves investing in the growth and development of our team members. As leaders, we have the privilege and responsibility to foster an environment that encourages continuous learning and personal development. This may include providing training opportunities, mentoring, and coaching, as well as creating a safe space for innovation and exploration. By investing in our team members' growth, we empower them to become leaders in their own right, ensuring the organization's long-term success and sustainability.

Guiding with responsibility also requires us to adopt a forward-thinking approach. We must be mindful of the long-term consequences of our decisions, both within the organization and in the broader context. By considering the impact on future generations, we make choices that are not solely driven by immediate gains but are sustainable and aligned with our values. This requires a willingness to adapt to changing circumstances, an openness to new ideas, and the ability to navigate uncertainty with resilience and agility.

Stewardship is a multidimensional aspect of servant leadership that requires us to embrace responsibility with integrity, compassion, and a long-term perspective. It involves the ethical use of resources, fostering a culture of accountability and transparency, engaging in community service, nurturing the growth of individuals, and making sustainable decisions. As servant leaders, we recognize our role as stewards and commit ourselves to make a positive impact, not only within our organizations but also in the larger world we live in. Our stewardship is an ongoing journey, continually evolving and adapting to the needs of those we serve and the challenges we face.

Commitment to Growth: Nurturing Talent and Potential

The commitment to growth is not only a crucial aspect but a deeply ingrained value. A servant leader understands that every individual possesses unique talents, abilities, and potential waiting to be nurtured and unleashed. By investing in the growth and development of others, they create a strong foundation for success, fostering a culture of continuous improvement, empowerment, and long-term sustainability. To effectively nurture talent and potential, servant leaders must first recognize and deeply believe in the capabilities of their team members.

They understand that each individual is imbued with a multitude of talents and that their potential goes beyond what meets the eye. Servant leaders have a keen ability to identify and appreciate the variety strengths that each team member brings to the table. They embrace the concept of multiple intelligences, understanding that intelligence is not limited to just academic or technical prowess. A servant leader recognizes and values the different intelligences present within their team, such as emotional intelligence, creative intelligence, and interpersonal intelligence.

A servant leader recognizes that growth and development are not limited to acquiring new skills or knowledge. They understand that personal growth entails a holistic approach that encompasses emotional, intellectual, and spiritual development. Servant leaders create an environment that encourages individuals to explore their vulnerabilities and step out of their comfort zones. They encourage self-reflection and provide opportunities for personal exploration, such as coaching, mindfulness practices, and self-assessment tools.

By nurturing the emotional and spiritual well-being of their team members, servant leaders enable them to flourish and reach their full potential. A servant leader knows that growth and development do not happen in isolation; they require a supportive network and community. Servant leaders actively seek opportunities to build a culture of collaboration and interdependence. They cultivate an environment where team members are encouraged to share knowledge, ideas, and experiences.

Through mentorship programs, cross-functional projects, and opportunities for peer-to-peer learning, servant leaders create a collaborative ecosystem that stimulates growth and promotes collective achievement. In addition to providing growth opportunities, servant leaders understand the importance of offering regular feedback and constructive guidance. They create spaces for conversations that focus on both recognizing achievements and addressing growth areas. Their feedback is specific, actionable, and delivered with empathy and respect, fostering an environment that facilitates individuals taking risks, learning from mistakes, and ultimately growing and excelling.

Servant leaders acknowledge that nurturing talent and potential is not limited to short-term goals but extends to long-term development. They invest time and effort in helping individuals identify their long-term aspirations and create personalized development plans. By providing guidance, support, and resources to help individuals reach their milestones, servant leaders demonstrate their commitment to the growth and success of their team members.

Commitment to growth surpasses the boundaries of conventional hierarchical roles. A servant leader recognizes that everyone has the capacity to lead and contribute to the growth of others. They foster an environment that encourages leadership at all levels, where team members are empowered to take ownership of their growth and development and support each other in reaching their goals. Servant leaders also understand that growth is not a linear path. It requires resilience, adaptability, and a commitment to lifelong learning.

Servant leaders model these qualities by continually seeking their own growth and development, acknowledging that they too have much to learn from their team members. This vulnerability and humility create an environment that values growth and inspires others to embrace a growth mindset. By nurturing talent and potential, servant leaders evoke a sense of purpose and fulfillment within their team members. They create a work environment where individuals feel valued, motivated, and empowered to unleash their full potential. This commitment to growth not only benefits the individuals themselves but also leads to increased engagement, loyalty, and ultimately, organizational success.

The commitment to growth is at the core of servant leadership. By recognizing the unique talents and potential of each individual, providing growth opportunities, offering feedback and guidance, and fostering a culture of continuous learning, servant leaders create an environment that nurtures talent and brings out the best in their team members. They lay the foundation for a future filled with empowered individuals who will carry the torch of servant leadership and make a significant impact on the world.

Building Community: Fostering Collaboration and Unity

In today's interconnected world, building a strong sense of community within organizations is not only desirable but essential for achieving collective goals and driving sustainable growth. A leader's role in this process goes beyond mere management; it is about creating an environment where individuals feel valued, connected, and invested in the shared purpose. At the heart of building a community is open communication and active listening.

A leader should be accessible and approachable, encouraging team members to voice their opinions, ideas, and concerns freely. Effective communication involves not just transmitting information, but also creating a space for dialogue, collaboration, and understanding. By establishing platforms for constructive conversations, such as team meetings, town halls, and informal check-ins, a leader ensures that ideas flow freely, and diverse perspectives are considered. Active listening plays a pivotal role in building strong interpersonal connections within the community. It goes beyond merely hearing the words spoken; it involves truly understanding the underlying emotions and intentions behind them.

A leader who actively listens demonstrates empathy, validating the emotions and experiences of others. This builds trust and rapport, making individuals feel seen and appreciated. To foster collaboration and unity, a servant leader cultivates a culture of psychological safety within the community. This means creating an atmosphere where individuals feel secure taking risks, expressing their true selves, and challenging conventional thinking. Leaders must demonstrate a willingness to receive feedback and admit their own mistakes, setting an example of humility.

Leaders should actively encourage ideas and suggestions from all team members, regardless of rank or position. In this environment, trust and empathy can flourish, paving the way for fruitful collaboration. Collaboration is not just about working together, but also about recognizing and leveraging the diverse strengths and perspectives of team members. A servant leader actively seeks input from individuals with different backgrounds, experiences, and skill sets. They understand that diversity brings a wealth of ideas and solutions, enriching the decision-making process and enhancing creativity. By fostering an environment where everyone's ideas are valued and respected, a leader encourages collaboration and teamwork, while ensuring that each person feels seen and heard.

In addition to promoting collaboration, a servant leader actively nurtures relationships among team members. They understand that strong social bonds have a profound impact on motivation, communication, and overall well-being. By organizing team-building activities, retreats, or even informal gatherings, a leader provides opportunities for individuals to connect on a personal level, fostering trust and camaraderie. Honest conversations, shared experiences, and celebrating both personal and professional achievements further strengthen the fabric of the community.

To create a truly cohesive community, a leader must champion a shared vision and purpose. By articulating the organization's mission, core values, and long-term goals, a leader inspires team members to connect their everyday work to something larger than themselves. When individuals understand how their contributions enhance and shape the broader vision, they feel a sense of purpose and motivation.

A servant leader continually communicates the vision, sharing stories of impact and success that further inspire and unite the community. Building a community is a continuous process that demands consistent effort and commitment from all members. A servant leader also leads by example, embodying the values and behaviors they seek from their team members. This helps strengthen the community because the leader's actions cultivate a culture of respect, and collaboration, consciously reinforcing these principles in their interactions, decision-making processes, and even performance evaluations.

By providing regular opportunities for feedback and recognizing and celebrating individual and team achievements, a leader ensures that the community remains vibrant, resilient, and responsive to change. A servant leader encourages a growth mindset within the community. They emphasize the importance of continuous learning and personal development, pushing team members to expand their skills and knowledge. By investing in professional development programs, mentorship opportunities, and cross-functional projects, a leader equips individuals with the tools and competencies they need to contribute meaningfully to the community's success.

A servant leader supports and encourages a healthy work-life balance, recognizing that individuals who feel fulfilled in both their professional and personal lives are more likely to be engaged, enthusiastic, and invested in the community. A servant leader understands the significance of recognizing and appreciating the contributions of team members. Regularly expressing gratitude and providing meaningful recognition strengthens individuals' sense of belonging and reinforces their commitment to the community. This recognition can take various forms, such as public acknowledgments, small gestures of appreciation, or opportunities for personal and professional growth.

Building a community founded on collaboration and unity is not a luxury. It is a necessity for thriving organizations in the modern world. A servant leader who prioritizes open communication, psychological safety, collaboration, relationship-building, alignment toward a shared vision, continuous learning, and recognition nurtures a community where team members are empowered to unleash their full potential and create remarkable outcomes together. Through their unwavering commitment to cultivating a strong sense of community, servant leaders pave the way for sustained success, resilience, and a brighter future.

Donning The Cloak of Servant Leadership

A Profound Journey

There comes a pivotal moment when one must fully embrace the role and essence of a servant leader. This stage is when leaders truly don the cloak of servant leadership and embody its principles, values, and practices to their core. At its heart, servant leadership is about a deep commitment to serving others, putting their needs before our own, and working tirelessly to create a nurturing environment where everyone can thrive. It is about shifting our mindset from a focus on power, authority, and control to one of humility, compassion, and empathy. It is a conscious choice to lead with integrity, authenticity, and a genuine desire to make a positive difference in the lives of those we lead.

The first step in donning the cloak of servant leadership is to wholeheartedly embrace the foundation of servant leadership: listening. True listening goes beyond passive hearing; it requires active engagement and a genuine desire to understand others. Leaders must cultivate the art of active listening, where they provide undivided attention, set aside judgments, and create a space where individuals feel encouraged to express themselves. By devoting our full attention and presence, we create an environment where individuals feel heard, valued, and respected. When leaders listen deeply, they gain insights into the true needs, concerns, and aspirations of their team members, enabling them to respond effectively and lead with empathy. From listening, we move to healing.

As servant leaders, we understand the importance of nurturing emotional well-being and supporting the personal growth of those we lead. We acknowledge and address the wounds and challenges individuals may carry, creating an environment where they feel supported and empowered to flourish. Servant leaders offer guidance, resources, and encouragement to help others overcome obstacles and reach their full potential.

Mindfulness and awareness are two other essential elements of donning the cloak of servant leadership. By cultivating presence and self-awareness, leaders become attuned to the present moment, their own emotions, and the needs of those around them. This heightened awareness allows them to respond skillfully and make well-informed decisions. Servant leaders make sure to foster a culture of mindfulness within their organizations, as well, encouraging team members to connect with their own inner wisdom, promoting clarity, focus, and resilience. Through mindfulness practices such as meditation, reflection, and purposeful pauses, servant leaders cultivate a sense of inner calm and equanimity that positively influences their interactions and decision-making.

Another aspect of donning the cloak of servant leadership is embracing the power of persuasion. Rather than relying solely on authority and coercion, servant leaders inspire and influence others through their values, vision, and passion. They engage in open and honest dialogue, encouraging participation and collaboration, leveraging their persuasive abilities to create a shared sense of purpose and commitment. This requires storytelling, effective communication, and the ability to articulate a compelling vision that resonates with the hearts and minds of those being led. Servant leaders excel at building relationships based on trust and mutual respect, allowing them to inspire others to take action aligned with the collective vision.

Conceptualization and foresight also play a critical role in servant leadership. Leaders must possess visionary thinking and the ability to envision a future that aligns with the organization's purpose and values. By thinking holistically and strategically, they anticipate and adapt to changes and challenges, inspiring confidence, trust, and forward-thinking action within their teams. Servant leaders not only create a clear direction but also communicate, contextualize, and align that vision with the values and aspirations of individuals and the organization as a whole. By involving others in the process of conceptualization, servant leaders harness the collective intelligence and creativity of their teams, fostering a sense of ownership and commitment to the shared vision.

Stewardship, the responsible and ethical management of resources and relationships, is a hallmark of servant leadership. Leaders must serve as diligent custodians, promoting the common good, and making decisions that prioritize the long-term well-being of all team members. This involves considering the impact of decisions and ensuring transparency, and accountability. By acting as stewards, servant leaders foster trust, transparency, and sustainability within their organizations, thereby nurturing an environment where everyone can thrive.

Stewards prioritize sustainability efforts, actively seek out ways to contribute to the betterment of society, and inspire others to do the same. Servant leadership is not a one-time act, but a commitment to continuous growth. Donning the cloak of servant leadership means investing in the development and growth of individuals, providing guidance, mentorship, and opportunities for them to reach their full potential. Servant leaders recognize the immense value of talent and actively cultivate an environment that nurtures and supports the growth of each team member. They facilitate learning, encourage experimentation, and celebrate both individual and collective achievements. Through ongoing learning and development opportunities, servant leaders foster a culture of excellence, innovation, and continuous improvement.

Donning the cloak of servant leadership calls on leaders to build a community, fostering collaboration, unity, and a sense of belonging. Servant leaders understand that collective efforts are more powerful than individual pursuits. By creating an inclusive and collaborative environment, they encourage diversity of thought, inspire teamwork, and forge strong bonds that drive organizational success. Servant leaders actively promote a culture of trust, respect, and appreciation, celebrating the uniqueness and contributions of each team member. They create platforms for open dialogue, encourage collaboration across teams and departments, and celebrate achievements as a collective, reinforcing a shared sense of purpose and creating an organizational ecosystem where collaboration and innovation thrive.

Donning the cloak of servant leadership is definitely a profound journey that requires a deep commitment to serving others while embodying principles of humility, compassion, and empathy. It encompasses active and empathic listening, cultivating mindfulness and awareness, persuasive communication, visionary thinking, responsible stewardship, nurturing growth, and fostering a sense of community. By fully embracing the essence of servant leadership and living its principles, leaders can profoundly impact the lives of others and create positive change in our world.

The grass is only green where it's watered, where it's given the things needed to thrive. Lead your team with a servant's heart and watch it thrive!

Epilogue: 4 Anecdotes of Servant Leaders in Action

Now, let's take a quick glimpse at some real-life examples of a few servant leaders who have left an indelible mark on the world. These people lived lives that showcased the principles and practices of servant leadership in action, demonstrating how they can have a transformative impact on individuals, organizations, and communities.

1. Mother Teresa:

Mother Teresa was born in Macedonia and was a Roman Catholic Nun. Eventually she would serve others in Ireland, as well as India. She was one of the first to establish homes for AIDS victims. In fact, she created homes for the poor and the dying literally all around the world. For more than 50 years, this courageous woman comforted the poor, the dying, and the unwanted all across the globe. Mother Teresa's greatest strengths as a leader was her relentless focus on her organization's mission: helping individuals in extreme need, the poorest of the poor.

2. Nelson Mandela:

Nelson Mandela made servanthood a driving force in his life, leadership, and legacy. And he changed the world. In every single thing he did, Mandela always made sure his actions helped the people he served. After his release from prison, Mandela negotiated with F.W. de Klerk to end apartheid. They accomplished this during racial tension and political instability. Consequently, they won the Nobel Peace prize for their efforts. Mandela eventually became the first black President of South Africa. He also changed the country by his selfless but determined leadership. Like the other greatest servant leaders, he possesses the essential trait of forgiveness.

3. Jack Welch:

Beloved former CEO of General Electric who wrote, "before you are a leader, success is all about growing yourself. When you become a leader, success is all about growing others." In Peter Drucker's classic HBR article on this topic, he noted that "executives spend more time on managing people and making people decisions than on anything else — and they should. No other decisions are so long lasting in their consequences or so difficult to unmake." Jack also believed this with all his heart and showed it in his leadership style. Another highlight of Jack's leadership was his extraordinary candor. He spoke bluntly and ensured his teams were always well informed. He was also insatiably curious, and encouraged his teams to be, too.

4. Herb Kelleher:

Former CEO of Southwest Airlines known for putting employees first. Kelleher worked hard to create a culture that inspired passionate people to come to work fully engaged, firing on all cylinders every day. He believed leaders needed to maintain a genuine interest in each of their employees, and he did so. He was approachable and he looked beyond titles and statuses. He believed in hiring for attitude and training for skill. Herb believed that employees should be treated like customers and celebrated for going above and beyond the call of duty. He explained it like this, "In business school, they'd say, 'This is a real conundrum: Who comes first, your employees, your shareholders, or your customers?' My mother taught me that your employees come first. If you treat them well, then they treat the customers well, and that means your customers come back and your shareholders are happy."

Resource Appendix

Below is a comprehensive list of resources that can help you delve deeper into the concepts and principles discussed throughout this book. These resources have been carefully selected to provide additional insights, practical tools, and further exploration of the topic of servant leadership.

Books:

"The Servant as Leader" by Robert K. Greenleaf:

This classic book by the founding father of servant leadership offers a foundational understanding of the theory and practice of this leadership approach. Greenleaf explores the idea that leaders should prioritize serving others first and how this can lead to increased trust, collaboration, and individual growth. This book serves as a starting point for anyone interested in servant leadership.

"The Power of Servant Leadership" by Robert K. Greenleaf and Larry C. Spears:

This collection of essays expands on Greenleaf's original work and explores various aspects of servant leadership. Through real-life examples, the authors illustrate how servant leaders can make a positive impact on individuals, organizations, and society as a whole. This book provides practical insights and encouraging stories that can inspire and guide aspiring servant leaders.

"Servant Leadership: A Journey into the Nature of Legitimate Power and Greatness" by Robert K. Greenleaf and Larry C. Spears:

This book presents a collection of speeches and essays that delve deeper into the principles and philosophy of servant leadership. It explores concepts such as empathy, healing, and persuasion as essential characteristics of servant leaders. This thought-provoking book invites readers to reflect on their own leadership styles and challenges them to adopt the servant leadership mindset.

"Leaders Eat Last: Why Some Teams Pull Together and Others Don't" by Simon Sinek:

Although not exclusively focused on servant leadership, this book explores the importance of leaders who prioritize the well-being of their team members. Sinek's insightful analysis reveals how creating a culture of trust and empathy can lead to increased loyalty, collaboration, and ultimately, success. By understanding the importance of serving others as a leader, readers will gain valuable insights into the application of servant leadership principles.

"The Servant Leader: How to Build a Creative Team, Develop Great Morale, and Improve Bottom-Line Performance" by James A. Autry:

Drawing from his own experiences as a business executive, Autry examines the key principles of servant leadership. He provides practical advice on how to foster a culture of service, build strong relationships with employees, and achieve sustainable success in the long run. This book offers actionable strategies and real-life examples that can inspire and guide leaders on their servant leadership journey.

"Dare to Serve: How to Drive Superior Results by Serving Others" by Cheryl Bachelder:

In this thought-provoking book, Bachelder shares her personal journey as a servant leader and demonstrates how this approach can transform both people and organizations. Through her experience as the CEO of Popeyes Louisiana

Kitchen, she shows how servant leadership can drive business growth, enhance employee engagement, and create a meaningful impact. This book offers practical insights, inspiring stories, and frameworks that can help leaders embrace and apply servant leadership principles.

Articles and Journals:

"The Power of Servant Leadership" by Ken Blanchard and Phil Hodges:

This article discusses the impact of servant leadership on performance and organizational culture. It highlights the importance of leaders who prioritize the needs of their team members, foster trust, and create a sense of purpose and belonging. The article provides research-based evidence and practical examples to demonstrate the positive influence of servant leadership.

"When and Why Power is Perceived as an Opportunity or a Threat: A Qualitative Study of Servant Leadership in the Workplace" by Lorna Doucet:

This research article explores the perceptions of power in the context of servant leadership. It dives into how servant leaders leverage their power to create positive outcomes, empower followers, and foster a culture of collaboration and growth. The article provides insights into the psychological dynamics of servant leadership and its implications for organizational success.

The Journal of Applied Behavioral Science:

This academic journal often features research and articles related to servant leadership and its application in various settings. Exploring articles in this journal can provide valuable insights into the latest research, trends, and best practices in servant leadership. It covers a wide range of topics, including servant leadership theory, measurement, applications, and training.

"Relational Leadership: A Call to Action for Servant Leaders" by Linda J. Crawford and Laura A. Pasquini:

This article explores the concept of relational leadership, which emphasizes building positive and authentic relationships with followers. It delves into how servant leaders can develop and leverage these relationships to promote collaboration, trust, and personal growth. The article also provides practical strategies for leaders to enhance their relational skills and cultivate a servant-led culture.

Online Courses and Workshops:

Servant Leadership Certification Program:

Offered by the Greenleaf Center for Servant Leadership, this program provides a comprehensive overview of servant leadership and offers practical tools for implementation. The program covers topics such as servant leadership philosophy, characteristics of servant leaders, and practical strategies for cultivating a servant-led culture. The certification program is designed to equip leaders with the knowledge and skills to become effective servant leaders in various contexts.

Leading with Servantship:

A free online course offered by the University of Notre Dame, this course explores the principles and practices of servant leadership. It examines the importance of empathy, humility, and active listening in leadership and provides practical guidance for integrating servant leadership into your own leadership style. This course offers interactive modules, case studies, and reflective exercises to support participants in developing their servant leadership capabilities.

Servant Leadership Workshop: Hosted by the Servant Leadership Institute, this immersive workshop offers a deep dive into the principles and practices of servant leadership. Participants will learn how to develop servant leadership skills, effectively communicate their vision, and create a culture that fosters trust, collaboration, and growth. The workshop combines interactive sessions, group exercises, and expert facilitation to provide a transformative learning experience.

Podcasts and Videos:

"The Servant Leadership Sessions" with James Strock:

In this podcast, James Strock explores the principles and practices of servant leadership through conversations with experts and thought leaders in the field. Each episode delves into different aspects of servant leadership, providing valuable insights and practical strategies for applying these principles in various contexts. The podcast covers a wide range of topics, from leadership in business and politics to personal development and social change.

"The Servant Leader Podcast" with Scott Maderer:

In this podcast, Scott Maderer interviews leaders from various industries who exemplify the principles of servant leadership. Through these conversations, listeners gain valuable insights into the mindset and practices of servant leaders. The podcast explores topics such as empathy, trust, and employee engagement, providing listeners with actionable tips and real-life examples to inspire their own leadership journey.

"The Power of Servant Leadership" with Amy Blaschka and Bill Fox:

In this video series, Amy Blaschka and Bill Fox interview leaders who have embraced servant leadership and experienced its transformative power. Through these conversations, viewers gain insights into the experiences and strategies of these leaders, as well as practical tips for integrating servant leadership principles into their own leadership practice. The videos provide valuable perspectives and inspirational stories that highlight the impact of servant leadership in diverse settings.

"Servant Leadership: The Power of Giving" TEDx Talk by Shelton Goode:

In this TEDx Talk, Shelton Goode explores the idea of servant leadership and its potential to create positive change in organizations and society. Drawing from his personal experiences, Goode shares how leaders who prioritize the needs of others foster a culture of trust, collaboration, and innovation. The talk encourages listeners to embrace the servant leadership mindset and consider the impact they can make by serving others and focusing on the greater good."

The Secret to Effective Leadership is Servant Leadership" TEDx Talk by Rick Christman:

In this TEDx Talk, Rick Christman discusses the concept of servant leadership and its importance in leading and inspiring others. Christman shares his own journey of discovering the power of servant leadership and provides practical examples of how leaders can create a positive impact by putting the needs of their team members first. The talk challenges traditional notions of leadership and encourages viewers to adopt a new approach that prioritizes service and collaboration.

These resources provide a wealth of knowledge and practical tools for individuals interested in deepening their understanding and practice of servant leadership. Whether through reading books, exploring articles, participating in workshops, or engaging with podcasts and videos, there are numerous avenues to continue the learning journey and develop as a servant leader. Remember that the true power of servant leadership lies in the application of its principles, so take what you learn and strive to integrate servant leadership into your own leadership practice.

About the Author

Michelle Murray is an author, screenwriter, thought leader, and advocate for servant leadership and personal development. Throughout her career in the United States Army and then leading her subsequent teams over a span of three decades, Michelle has endeavored to inspire individuals to discover their true potential, lead with compassion, and make a positive impact on the world around them.

Michelle Murray is a native Texan. She is a combat Veteran of the United States Army. She held a variety of leadership assignments as an Air Defense Soldier, including being a test candidate for the Stinger Missile program when consideration was given to opening it up to women, and she was one of the only female Air Defense Artillery Soldiers to jump with the Golden Knights. She also served as the Brigade Adjutant for the world's largest Air Defense Artillery Brigade, the 11th Air Defense Artillery Brigade.

Prior to a career in the United States Army, Michelle was a member of the Ft Worth Police Department's Weed and Seed Division, an arm of the federal drug task force of the same name. She had the pleasure of also being a part of the department's Kid's Code Blue Program, a program which helped rehabilitate juvenile offenders and provide opportunities to at-risk youth. Additionally, a fun fact is that she mentored thousands of elementary aged children while working as the mascot McGruff the crime dog.

In addition to being COO of KMP Entertainment, she now enjoys hobbies that include: SCUBA Diving, camping, hiking, horse-back riding, a few sports, and extensive travel.

Her most recent novels are available in both e-book and traditional formats wherever books are sold.

Michelle's resume credits also include Fox's The Cleaning Lady, Will Smith's Netflix movie "Bright", and Season One, Episode 13 of the CBS show "Man With a Plan," "Crazy Ones," with Robin Williams and "The Mentalist." Additionally, you can follow her on Newsbreak for news delivery that is always based in fact and never emotion.

Michelle is a certified Life Coach, with specialization in NLP (Neuro-linguistic Programming Techniques, and REBT (Rational Emotive Behavioral Techniques) Mindset coaching. She truly helps her clients empower their beliefs and have (or take back) control of their lives.

Also of note, Michelle was the 2019 Ms. North Hollywood title holder for the Ms. California Plus Pageant, and the 2023 Miss California Queen of Charity title holder. She is a Rotarian, and avid community volunteer. Michelle holds a Bachelor degree in Entertainment Business and a Master of Fine Arts degree in Creative Writing. She is currently wrapping up work on her Doctorate.

Michelle enjoys hearing from readers. You can contact her/give her feedback by emailing her at info@kmpentertainment.org If you would like to review this book, or any of her others, please leave a review on Barnes and Noble, Walmart, Amazon or other retailer pages.

You can keep up with Michelle's projects by going to her company's website www.kmpentertainment.org or via Facebook at the KMP Entertainment page, https://www.facebook.com/KMPEntertainment/

www.ingramcontent.com/pod-product-compliance
Lightning Source LLC
Chambersburg PA
CBHW060354130626
46553CB00003B/1222